## SPORTS FOR FUN AND FITNESS

# MARTIAL ARTS
# FOR FUN AND FITNESS

**Enslow Publishing**
101 W. 23rd Street
Suite 240
New York, NY 10011
USA

enslow.com

**Jeff Mapua**

Published in 2020 by Enslow Publishing, LLC.
101 W. 23rd Street, Suite 240, New York, NY 10011

**Library of Congress Cataloging-in-Publication Data**

Names: Mapua, Jeff, author.
Title: Martial arts for fun and fitness / Jeff Mapua.
Description: New York : Enslow Publishing, 2020 | Series: Sports for Fun and Fitness | Audience: Grade level for this book is K-4. | Includes bibliographical references and index.
Identifiers: LCCN 2019004740| ISBN 9781978513433 (library bound) | ISBN 9781978513419 (paperback) | ISBN 9781978513426 (6 pack)
Subjects: LCSH: Martial arts for children--Juvenile literature. | Physical fitness--Juvenile literature.
Classification: LCC GV1101.35 .M26 2019 | DDC 796.8--dc23
LC record available at https://lccn.loc.gov/2019004740

Printed in the United States of America

**To Our Readers**: We have done our best to make sure all website addresses in this book were active and appropriate when we went to press. However, the author and the publisher have no control over and assume no liability for the material available on those websites or on any websites they may link to. Any comments or suggestions can be sent by email to customerservice@enslow.com.

**Photo Credits:** Martial Arts – Research by Bruce Donnola

Cover, p. 1 (martial arts athletes) artpipi/E+/Getty Images; cover and interior pages (balls and birdie) Lightspring/Shutterstock.com; p. 7 Kaderov Andrii/Shutterstock.com; p. 9 Iakov Filimonov/Shutterstock.com; p. 10 Design Pics Inc/Alamy Stock Photo; p. 13 © iStockphoto.com/Ridofranz; p. 15 Ilike/Shutterstock.com; p. 16 © iStockphoto.com/7stock; p. 18 © iStockphoto.com/KatarzynaBialasiewicz; p. 20 Michael Ochs Archives/Moviepix/Getty Images; p. 21 Ververidis Vasilis/Shutterstock.com; p. 23 7stock/iStock/Getty Images; p. 26 Karl Johaentges/LOOK/Getty Images; p. 28 © iStockphoto.com/miljko

# Contents

# Introduction

Action movies are exciting to watch. Many have incredible scenes where two or more characters fight each other. The actors move quickly and look like blurs on the screen. Sometimes the fights start to look like dances. Movies today use martial arts to entertain people.

The 1984 film *The Karate Kid* is a famous martial arts movie. Karate is a form of martial art. The movie is about a boy named Daniel who moves to a new city. Without any friends, he meets a man who teaches him karate. Through karate, Daniel begins a new life in his new city. He eventually finds friends and earns the respect of his classmates at school.

The movie ends with a memorable scene. In it, Daniel fights his way to the end of a tournament. In a fight against his bully, Daniel performs "the crane kick." People who saw the movie began imitating the kick in real life. The movie's producer Jerry Weintraub said, "When I came out of the first screening of *The Karate Kid*, there were a hundred kids in the parking lot doing the crane kick." The movie went on to be a major blockbuster.

But martial arts can be more than just great entertainment. It can be a great way to get into shape, too. Like dancing, martial arts get people moving around. Punches and kicks build muscle strength. They also build up **stamina** and **endurance**. Martial arts students also learn how to keep balance. Over time, people who learn martial arts gain better control of their own bodies.

Students learn how to practice with one another. This includes **sparring**, or making the motions without hitting too hard. Sparring is a great way to interact with others in a respectful way. There's much more to martial arts than the crane kick.

# CHAPTER 1

## A Positive Activity

**M**artial arts are a physical activity that often involve one person trying to knock their opponent down before they themselves are knocked down. There is punching, kicking, jumping, and much more involved. There is more than one type of martial art, too. Each style of martial arts focuses on different parts of physical fitness.

Martial arts are a variety of disciplines taught to improve one's control of mind and body.

## Strength Training

Adding strength helps a person add power to their martial arts moves. This means punches and kicks hit harder. It also means that a person is less likely to get injured, because their body is strong.

As people train in martial arts, they build muscle. It is true no matter what style people learn. Building muscle also helps develop bone mass. More bone mass helps avoid problems such as easily broken bones.

Practicing moves in slow motion helps build strength. For example, performing kicks in slow motion helps build the leg muscles. It is important for martial artists to build strength without losing flexibility.

## Flexibility

A flexible person can bend and stretch their body without hurting themselves. Martial arts help increase a person's flexibility. Doing so helps avoid injuries like strained or

## TAE BO

Tae Bo was a fitness craze in the 1990s. It combined tae kwon do with other workout styles. People could buy videos of the creator, Billy Blanks, showing viewers how to work out. The craze showed that martial arts could be a great way to get fit.

Stretching helps warm up your muscles and prepare them for more complicated movements.

sprained joints and muscles. It also allows a person to perform amazing things in martial arts. A person with flexible legs can kick higher. Their movements will be smoother than someone with stiff muscles.

Training in martial arts means having to stretch often. Full-body stretches are a good idea. It is recommended that stretches be done slowly and smoothly. For example, a person can stretch by sitting on the floor with one leg

Balance is an important part of all martial arts. Can you stand on one leg without falling over?

extended straight out. They then slowly and smoothly reach out and try to touch their toes. This position should be held for at least ten seconds. Bouncing should be avoided, as it might injure the muscle.

# Balance

People may overlook balance, but it is a big part of physical fitness. A physically fit person will be able to stand on one leg without falling over. Martial arts help people develop a good sense of balance. Good balance will also help people kick higher and throw more powerful punches. Being able to stay standing is an important skill when performing martial arts.

One way to learn balance is to be knocked off balance. For example, students can lean too far one way then try to keep themselves from falling. Another trick is to maintain balance with closed eyes.

# CHAPTER 2

In Control

**M**artial arts are not only for physical fitness. They are a great way to build mental fitness as well. Many styles of martial arts encourage working on both the mind and body.

## Focus

The ability to **focus** is important in martial arts and in everyday life. Being able to pay attention to a particular thing helps people accomplish tasks and reach goals.

Martial arts may help you learn how to focus on
other parts of your life, like schoolwork.

Research has shown that better focus and control leads
to stronger punches and kicks.

Studies have also shown that practicing martial arts
even leads students to better grades in math. People
who study martial arts are found to be more alert, with

## BECOME BETTER PEOPLE

Mark Moore is a karate instructor and owner of Underground Martial Arts Fitness Center in New Jersey. He teaches karate to both kids and adults. However, his students learn more than just martial arts. Twelve-year-old Kirsten Bradford said, "He teaches us about self-respect, self-control, to be respectful to others, how to be a good student, and encourages us to volunteer."

improved attention. They have better control over their bodies and minds.

Researchers believe that better focus comes from sparring. A person sparring needs to pay close attention to their opponent. Doing so helps them avoid punches and kicks coming their way.

## Self-Control

Martial arts help people learn to control their **emotions**. This means that people do not lose control of their feelings. For example, people can get too angry when something bad happens. People who have self-control don't allow themselves to become too angry and do something foolish because of their emotions.

When you're angry, it's hard to do anything right. Martial arts can help you control your anger.

Self-control is helpful in competition. Many people participate in martial arts tournaments. Being able to control their emotions gives people a better chance at winning. Losing self-control means not being in control of one's punches and kicks.

Self-control is similar to **self-discipline**. Self-discipline is something you can learn, just like martial arts. If you learn your weaknesses, you can turn them into strengths. This takes practice, just like any sport does. Self-discipline is doing your homework when you would rather ride your bike.

As you learn to control your body, you can also learn to control your mind, emotions, and reactions to the world around you.

## Mind and Body

The body can be trained to become stronger. People can strengthen their minds to have better focus and self-control. Martial arts are a way to both strengthen the body and the mind. Training connects a person's mind and body.

Many styles of martial arts teach students to meditate. Meditation is thinking deeply and focusing one's mind in silence. It is a way to reduce stress and promote happiness. Meditating is often done sitting in a comfortable position with eyes closed. Focusing on breathing is an important part. Just a few minutes a day can be helpful.

# CHAPTER 3

Like Water

**B**y definition, martial arts involve self-defense and attack. People learn how to handle themselves when faced with conflict or disagreements.

## Conflict Resolution

**Conflict resolution** is the ability to find a peaceful solution to a disagreement between two or more people. Martial arts help develop this particular skill. Students in martial arts learn how to properly defend themselves when physically attacked. However, the idea is to

Martial arts isn't a team sport like many others, but it can still teach you how to work with people.

learn how to do those things in order to not use them. Nonviolent conflict resolution is the ultimate goal.

Neil Kagan is an eighth-degree kung fu master. He has been practicing kung fu for 40 years and has been teaching for three decades. Kagan points out that kung fu, like other styles and disciplines, teaches students to stop a fight before it starts. He says, "You learn it's not all about the physical fighting." It is not about violence. "I teach you to be able to stand up to anybody," Kagan told *The Business Observer* in Florida in a 2018 interview. "The greatest soldier wins without a battle, so that's what we practice and what we teach."

The ability to peacefully resolve conflicts comes from a strong sense of self-confidence. Self-confidence is the feeling or belief in oneself. People who study martial arts develop the ability to handle conflict while it is happening.

## BRUCE LEE AND WATER

Bruce Lee was a legendary martial artist. He developed his own style called Jeet Kune Do. He considered his style as "formless." This meant that there were no boundaries to his style. "Be formless, shapeless like water," Lee said. "Now you put water into a cup, it becomes the cup. You put water into a bottle, it becomes the bottle. Put it in a teapot, it becomes the teapot. Water can flow, water can crash. Be water, my friend."

Bruce Lee was a master of martial arts, introducing
the world to his craft in the movies he made.

## Keep on Ticking

In martial arts, students learn how to take a hit. This
could be a punch, kick, throw, or other form of attack.
Half of martial arts is hitting while the other half is taking a hit. No one can go without ever getting hit during

training or practice. This is true in both martial arts and in life. Martial arts teach students that it is okay to fail.

Learning how to take hits helps people relax and better protect themselves. Some teachers even encourage their students to let themselves be hit right away in a sparring match. The idea is to understand that getting hit is not the end of the world. People learn to take a hit and get back up.

In martial arts, you will learn how to deliver strikes, but also how to take them, all without being injured.

# CHAPTER 4

## The Art of Choice

There are many styles of martial arts to choose from. Learning what each is about can lead to a more rewarding experience.

### Karate

Karate is a style of martial arts that began in Okinawa, Japan. It means "empty hand." Weapons are not

There are many different kinds of martial arts, each with a different focus. Pick which one works best for you!

commonly taught. Chinese **techniques** influenced its early development. Modern karate began around 1700 CE, but different features of karate started as early as 1000 BCE.

Students of karate mark their progress with different colors of belts. Everyone begins as a white belt. The final belt is black. There are ten levels of black belt.

Karate teaches students to focus one's strength in the small, bony areas of the fist and foot. Attacks utilize the entire body. Speed is a big part of the style. Karate is considered a "hard" style. Many movements are straightforward, such as punches and kicks.

Karate teaches using an opponent's movements against them. For example, an opponent's attacks are redirected so they lose balance.

## Kung Fu

Shaolin monks developed kung fu in China. Many stories credit a man named Bodhidharma as the inventor of kung fu around 520 CE. Kung fu techniques began

## OTHER STYLES

Judo is a Japanese style. Instead of punches and kicks, it focuses on throws and taking the opponent to the ground. Krav Maga is an Israeli combat system that can be described as intense and is done with minimum wasted effort. Mixed martial arts, or MMA, combines different styles of martial arts, including boxing.

to develop around 1000 BCE. The goal of kung fu is to overcome oneself, not an opponent.

Kung fu is considered a "soft" style. The style is more graceful than hard styles. Many movements are circular. Kung fu teaches the use of weapons. These include swords, short and long sticks, **nunchaku** or nunchuck, *sai*, and more. Blocks often redirect attacks rather than meeting force with force.

Kung fu is considered more graceful than other martial arts and has many moves named after animals.

There are a variety of styles and techniques. Many are named after animals. A kung fu student may learn crane, tiger, dragon, or other styles. Traditional kung fu does not use a belt system.

## Tae Kwon Do

Tae kwon do, sometimes spelled taekwondo, is a Korean martial art. The English meaning of the words is "the way of the foot and fist." It is an official sport in the Olympics. The style developed over the course of 2,300 years in Korea. Tae kwon do is a union of five major Korean martial arts academies.

Tae kwon do is different from other styles because of the focus on high kicks. The idea is to take advantage of how much longer legs are than arms. Kicks are often combined with spinning and jumping. Hand techniques emphasize fast movements. Tae kwon do teaches the use of weapons. These include nunchaku, swords, spears, and more.

Tae kwon do focuses on high kicks, to take advantage of how long a person's legs are. How high can you kick?

## The Journey Begins

It is best to first see what schools are available. A style may not be taught in every town or city. Choosing a good teacher is also an important factor. Once a style is selected, the journey toward a healthy mind and body can truly begin.

# Words to Know

**conflict resolution**   The ability to find a peaceful solution to a disagreement between two or more people.

**emotion**   A person's mental state and feelings.

**endurance**   The ability to exert yourself for long periods of time.

**focus**   To pay particular attention.

**nunchaku**   A weapon made of two sticks connected by a short chain or rope.

**sai**   A dagger with two sharp prongs curving outward from the hilt.

**self-discipline**   The ability to overcome emotions to do what is believed to be right.

**sparring**   Making the motions of attack and defense as a part of training.

**stamina**   Enduring energy, strength, and resilience.

**technique**   The way of carrying out the technical skills of a martial art.

# Learn More

## Books

Casarella, Antonello, and Roberto Ghetti. *A Complete Guide to Kung Fu.* New York, NY: Enslow Publishing, 2018.

Marino, Stefano Di, and Roberto Ghetti. *A Complete Guide to Karate.* New York, NY: Enslow Publishing, 2018.

O'Farrell, Eamonn. *Martial Arts.* Harlow, UK: Pearson Education, 2016.

## Websites

**The American Academy of Pediatrics**
*healthychildren.org*
The American Academy of Pediatrics (AAP) educates families about the healthy way to pursue martial arts and other forms of exercise.

**Bruce Lee Foundation**

*bruceleefoundation.org*

The Bruce Lee Foundation encourages a healthy lifestyle that aligns mind, body, and spirit through the use of Bruce Lee's philosophies.

**Kids Web Japan**

*web-japan.org/kidsweb/*

Kids can learn about all things Japan including karate and other Japanese martial arts.

# Index